CELEBRATE LIFE'S MIRACLES

Pondering the Signs of Love

To Mary.

Patti Rae Fletcher

Keep Noticing your
Fabulous Miracles

Love ~

Patti Rae
Fletcher

ISBN 978-1-7326522-6-2

Published by Summit Street Publishing
131 West Grand River
Owosso, Michigan 48867

The author of this book does not dispense medical advice or prescribe the use of any technique as a form of treatment for physical, emotional, or medical problems without the advice of a physician, either directly or indirectly. The intent of the author is only to offer information of a general nature to help you in your quest for emotional and spiritual well-being. In the event you use any of the information in this book for yourself, which is your constitutional right, the author and the publishers assume no responsibility for your actions.

The photographs within the pages are the authors own photography.

Library of Congress Cataloging-in-Publication data
Fletcher, Patti Rae
Celebrate Life's Miracles / Patti Rae Fletcher -1st ed.

CELEBRATE LIFE'S MIRACLES is the second book of memoirs by Patti Rae Fletcher.
All names have been changed to protect the privacy of individuals in this book.
Cover art by Mitchell Scheidel
Cover design by Emily E. Lawson
Edited by Debbie R. McGinnis

Dedication

To my husband, sons, and granddaughter… You keep me balanced, and without balance, I would not exist as who I am. I love and treasure you all, forever and always.

Contents

Acknowledgements

How do you acknowledge extraordinary, priceless gifts?

To all those who have been brave enough to share their inner authentic selves and sacred experiences with me... You have influenced my thoughts, beliefs and have impacted my life.

I'm so grateful to and for the people and places that have magically shown up in my life—all in perfect timing.

My loving, compassionate reflexologist Lily, along with several knowledgeable physical therapists, a wonderful masseuse, and all those who choose to be in the medical field. Your gifts of love and compassion have made a monumental difference in this world and have been invaluable to me, my mind, body, and spirit—my thoughts, physical health, and authentic self. You all have my forever gratitude and love.

And as an extra bonus—the Universe surprised me with an amazing editor for this book, Debbie R. McGinnis. You are the epitome of kindness and professionalism. Thank you!

Introduction

As in my previous book, *This Sign Was Mine—Message Received!* Each chapter relates to a unique life-changing experience I've had. The Universe continues to supply special messages to help me move forward in any circumstance through this miraculous life. I believe this to be true for all humankind.

With my many recent life events—one that includes a health diagnosis that none of us want to hear—I'm still assured that I'm never alone. I have been poked and prodded by something way more powerful than myself, or any doctor, to share these out-of-the-ordinary signs, marvels, miracles, and what I feel are divine connections with you once again. At the end of each chapter, I've included questions to ponder that will hopefully help you become more aware and curious about your own life signs, nudges, messages, and miraculous connections.

A long time ago, I received a game for Christmas called *Concentration*. It's a matching game that later became a popular television show. The player chose two numbered tiles from a board. If they matched when they were turned over, a hidden snippet of a rebus puzzle would be revealed. The object of the game was to recognize and reveal the puzzle to complete the hidden message or phrase. At times, the solution was clear early in the game and I'd know the answer to the whole puzzle. However, other times I didn't understand the picture until more of the game board had been uncovered. Sometimes I couldn't get it until I could see the entire rebus picture. The answers, messages, or warnings I receive from the Universe are comparable with the way that once-popular game was played.

Certain signs and messages are clear in an instant, and I know the answers right away. Other times I must open myself to the knowing that all will be revealed in the right time with what tiny bit of information or clues I've been shown.

Signs can come in a plethora of simple thoughts, ideas, or a-ha moments. They can appear as dreams, special hugs or perhaps song lyrics—the ones that connect to only you. They can be pictures, scents, certain sensations like tingles, vibrations, or chill bumps. I like to call them angel bumps. These things can trigger a deep-seeded emotional and/or spiritual healing, lead you in a specific direction or maybe let you know that a deceased loved-one is near. You will know the truth when you feel it inside. Trust your intuition.

By paying attention to your thoughts—a new idea, quick question, a person's image, name, or something that seems coincidental pops into your mind—try to remember that it's important to pause and ponder what happened in that moment? How did it make you feel? Did you think of a loved one? Why? Was there a message for you there or was it simply meant to lift your spirits? If you get a strange feeling about something or someone don't just blow it off as a freak happening or coincidence. Think about it.

One of my joy signs comes when an airplane flies close overhead, close enough for me to feel the vibration of its powerful engines throughout the vehicle I'm in. This incident never fails to raise tiny bumps on my arms and always prompts a thought of my dad. I feel his warm loving comfort and can envision him sitting in the driver's seat, his smile takes over his entire face and he's filled with true bliss.

The memory of Dad and I parked near the airport becomes vivid. We would do this often throughout my childhood. We'd watch the planes take off and land for an hour or two. He was a man of few words. However, during every airport visit, he'd say, "Can you believe it? How can all that steel rise in the air like it was as light as a feather?" This memory comes to my mind every time I am close enough to feel, hear, or see a low-flying plane. I trust the words that come to my mind as my eyes fill. *Yes, Dad I'm thinking of you too. Thank you for still watching over me.* I chuckle to myself as our game continues with my same question—*So Dad, are the planes as fun to watch from the top view as they were from underneath?* I sense his quiet presence and special grin as I feel the vibrations of the planes.

In recent months I've come to believe that sometimes our thoughts, signs or messages aren't always to help us, but perhaps we are being nudged to help others. We never know what impact we can have on the people around us with a bit of unplanned kindness, with our words or in our actions. I've silently asked myself on several occasions, *Why did I say or do that?* Yet I've come to understand that it was exactly what another person needed in that instant.

When I take the time to ruminate on past situations, goals, dreams, and the adversities in life, even though some can be emotionally painful, I've learned to recognize the synchronicities that have taken place. I have been replenished by the miracles and will always remember the sensations of comfort and love received in those exact moments when I needed them. It makes me realize our trials and tribulations in the past and present in our daily life are when each amazing miracle comes upon us. One "a-ha" moment for me was when I finally realized that we are not in control as much as we'd like to believe. I'm thankful for this. It is a freeing thought to be willing to surrender.

Heart shapes are paramount in my previous book and they still find their way to me almost daily. I see them wherever I am. Hearts never fail to fill my soul with joy and to remind me of the unconditional love of my parents. Besides finding heart-shapes in the sky, and on the ground, and in the trees—even on the fur of some animals—they have recently shown up on my body. However, my favorite heart shapes are the ones that appear in the zaniest and most unexpected places.

A Recent Example

As I returned to my car after a hair appointment, I spotted a tiny jagged heart-shape halfway up the building where the paint had weathered away. The people that own this salon are spiritual, loving human beings. My heart and smile grew as I thought that even their business building displays their love. That's the way I want to live my life, exuding love. Of course, by my next appointment, the heart-shape on the building had changed and now resembled a messy blob. I wondered if I had been the only person to notice how the universal sign of love took shape on their place of business.

Even with my history of proof that the Universe is guiding me with perfectly timed synchronicities—and has been all my life—I still question on occasion. To trust what I see, feel, and hear in my thoughts or words spoken aloud is an ongoing process for me. I still have much to learn, but I'm getting there. I am more alert about what's going on within, what I'm thinking and how I'm feeling physically and mentally —and why.

Because of my recent health scare, I have become even more aware of several of my transitioned loved ones being by my side. I understood their signs, felt their presence, and have even heard their words of comfort. I also believe they created lifesaving interventions with several of my living loved ones. I didn't need to fear anything. The signs were accurate and filled me with that extraordinary cozy comfort and divine unconditional love as usual, all in the Universe's perfect timing. I'm so grateful!

If you were drawn to this book, I believe there is a reason. My hope is that after reading about these experiences, you will recognize your own synchronicities, signs, and messages, so that you can live your life with hope, inspiration, joy, and fulfillment.

Now, on to the miracles of life that seemed to line up in divine order. They showed me how synchronicities made it possible for me to still be here so that I can share these ethereal experiences with you.

Chapter 1

The Heart House

"A house could be filled with things that will eventually be emptied; however, a home that has been filled with love will leave an infinite impression." ~ P.R. Fletcher

In my previous book, I wrote about the day before my dad's funeral. It was a frigid February afternoon; however, the sun was bright, and the sidewalks were free from ice. I walked outdoors in hopes of lessening my devastation. I came upon a perfectly timed, miraculous sign from the Universe—its message twinkling clear.

I had paused on a street corner to catch my breath and blow my nose. When I raised my eyes, I couldn't believe what I saw. I wiped my face and stared across the street again. An instant infusion of delight zipped through my body. It was the first time I had smiled in days. There was an almost perfectly formed ten-foot heart shape that was made of snow on a second-story rooftop.

In the sun, the heart appeared to be created of diamonds that glistened like none I'd ever seen. I wanted to run up to that person's door, drag them to the street, and show them the shape on their roof, but something held me in place. I felt this sign had been singled out for me at this moment, at this time of desperate need and unbearable woefulness.

As the wintery breeze hit my face, tranquility and love replaced the tension and nervous energy that had moments before twitched through my entire body. This calm consumed my whole being, as if a hot-out-of-the-dryer, super-soft fuzzy blanket had been draped around my body. I'm not sure how long I stood on that sidewalk in front of a stranger's home and stared, but at that moment, I had no doubt that I would make it through the funeral—and the next day, and the next, and eventually the rest of my life.

My heart-shaped signs have continued to show up through the years. I see them everywhere now. I know deep-down in my soul that they represent the unconditional love of my parents for me and the reminder to give as well as to be open to receive that same sort of love.

Since that day, I've called it 'the Heart House.'

My Heart House is about a mile from my home, so I pass it every day on my walks. When I see it, I wonder things like, *Why that house? Why that moment? Who lives there? Do they have any idea what a special house they live in?* One that gives tangible signs of love... Only once in five years did I happen by when someone was outside.

It turns out that the Heart House has a spirit filled love story of its own. I somehow knew it would.

Recently, while on my daily walk about a half-block away from the Heart House, I saw a car pull into the driveway. I told myself if the occupant was out of the car by the time I walked by, I would be brave enough to introduce myself. I quickened my pace and felt a burst of confident energy race through my body.

By the time I reached the house, the lady in the car had already gone through the gate toward her side door and I thought, *Oh well, there will be another time.* But as I started to pass, I heard the gate creak open and saw the woman returning to her car. I hurried back as she opened the trunk to retrieve something. I held out my hand and said, "Hi, I'm Patti Rae. Are you the homeowner here?"

She nodded with a bit of hesitation and shook my hand. "I'm Arlene."

I'm sure my words ran together like one long run-on sentence as they rolled off my tongue. "You're probably going to think I'm crazy, but I literally wrote a story about your house, and I've never been the same since. I refer to your home as my Heart House." She raised one eyebrow and cocked her head a bit. I continued, "And here's why..." I relayed the story of my devastation the day before Dad's funeral and the snow heart.

When I finished, she held my gaze a moment and nodded, "Well," she said, "now it's your turn to think *I'm* nuts." She waved her hand toward the house and said, "The house was built in the 1930s and I'm only the second owner. After the original homeowners passed away, the house went to the bank and sat empty for many years." Arlene explained that she had signed the final papers of purchase and had become the new homeowner in 1996.

She'd cleaned the house from top to bottom to make it her own and lastly went up into the attic. This is where Arlene had discovered a tattered cardboard box filled with wedding pictures from the original owners' special day. She contacted the bank to see if they could locate any family members, and she was told that the couple didn't have children or any living relatives. They advised her to pitch the box, but her heart ached at the thought. She just couldn't bring herself to throw away those stunning photos representing the couple's life-long marriage.

Arlene said, "This couple, even in their photographs, seemed to exude love. The photographer had done his or her job well. Love could be seen in their eyes, and bright smiles."

Arlene said she felt like she could sense their joy as she traced her fingers along several of the aged, fragile photographs. She had delicately sorted through the box of historic treasures and chosen her favorite picture of the couple to put into a unique, old-fashioned frame that she hoped suited the times. It still hangs above her fireplace to this day. Love everlasting!

"Sometimes," Arlene said softly, "in the late evenings, I hear whispers."

"Wow, do you think it's the couple?"

"It's sounds like a female and a male voice. I can't make out the words, but what other explanation is there?" Arlene chuckled, then asked, "So now do you think *I'm* nuts?"

"Absolutely not," I said as I felt that familiar tingling, calm sensation run through my body. I'd known five years before that there was something extraordinary about that house. On that day, I knew in my soul that it was a true-love house.

I reached out my hand once again and said, "It truly has been my pleasure to meet you after all these years. It means a lot that you shared your home's history with me. I'll drop off a copy of my book, *This Sign was Mine, Message Received!* on my next walk, so you can see the photograph of the snow heart on your roof. Thank you for talking with me."

"You're welcome," she said as she grabbed my hand.

I felt grateful to finally have met Arlene. What an extraordinary conversation and a wonderful deepening to my Heart House experience—and yet another element to validate her home's history and its own love story. I stood on the next corner, glanced back at the house, and thought, *A house could be filled with things that will eventually be emptied; however, a home that has been filled with love will leave an infinite impression.*

Arlene's wasn't the first story I'd heard about spirits or someone hearing voices. I've had my own experiences with messages and signs from deceased loved ones. And if it hadn't been for all those past experiences, I never would have believed that some of my health support and encouragement could come from the beyond.

The best part of meeting Arlene was that neither one of us thought the other was bonkers.

PONDER: Have you ever encountered something so extraordinary that it felt unexplainable? But you knew there was something... You felt it inside. Take time to question the occurrence. When did you feel it? What did you see, hear, or feel in those moments? What was the thought connected to the circumstance? Had you been thinking about something before the situation? Has anyone you have ever known spoken of a spirit or angel experience?

Chapter 2

Divine Hugs

"There are times, when I recognize a spirit soul can embrace the soul of another while in human form." ~ P.R. Fletcher

This is a chapter that didn't make it into, *This Sign Was Mine,* I worked with it, revised it, and rewrote it several times then realized it was meant for another place, another time, or possibly another book. I'd had only two spiritual embraces at that time and the chapter simply didn't feel complete. I set it aside. Maybe I'd be lucky enough to have another one, and three would be the magic number. I have since discovered that perhaps there is no magic number for certain things, especially those that are not in our control, and I am grateful.

I've received possibly millions of hugs in my life from family, friends, loved ones, and a few complete strangers, and they were all nice, important, and most have been welcomed. However, three of these hugs remain enshrined in my soul, never to be forgotten.

They came with something even more powerful than physical touch and comfort from the outside. I feel they were spiritual gifts, way above and beyond a casual hug. On the occasions these special embraces occurred, I was at the point of extreme mental devastation, not knowing how I was going to get through the next moments without losing my mind, let alone days, weeks, and months. I feel these special people were in the perfect place, at the perfect time, in the perfect moment, where anything else besides these divine hugs would not have served me in the healing or confidence I needed to carry on.

Two of the people who gave me hugs seemed highly unlikely to reach out to me with an embrace. Divine timing? Yes! Synchronicity? Yes! Coincidence? No! The people followed their intuition, their inner guidance, and synchronicity brought us together in perfect timing.

Their hugs being providential for me makes me wonder if they felt anything as special or as extraordinary as I did at the time? Something inside says the Universe may have set up some twofers.

The first hug came almost two decades ago from someone I had only seen and never had spoken to. It happened when my father-in-law had experienced a massive heart attack followed by multiple mini strokes. He wasn't expected to live. The hospital contacted the family on several occasions to come and say their farewells.

My husband did his best to stay strong for his mom and siblings. He stayed mostly at the hospital as I remained in our home to take care of our family and everything that needed to be done there. Part of me wanted to be with them, because waiting for detailed information from the intensive care unit can be more challenging than being there, especially when there are medical changes every few minutes. We were all stressed and handling things in our own ways. But just because I wasn't with the immediate family at the hospital daily, spending the nights, and speaking with the medical teams, doesn't mean I wasn't hurting for my wonderful father-in-law, my husband, and all my in-laws.

This gentle, generous human being, the father of the wonderful man I married, had a way of making me feel accepted as one of his own, without exception. His kindness was absolute, and his brilliant smile was one of those so genuine you could feel it all the way to your toes. It truly touched me every time we saw one another. His happiness was always apparent without him ever saying a word.

On Sunday, I attended church alone with a lack of sleep and a ton of built up emotions. After the service, feeling so useless, I made a last-second decision to hurry into the parish office to ask for special prayers for my father-in-law and our family.

I stood at the doorway, gripping the doorframe for support. I struggled with the dry lump in my throat. No words came at first. The dark-haired woman behind the desk—the Director of Religious Education at the time—raised her head from her paperwork. Her eyes widened as she saw me. I must have been a sight, pale and on the verge of tears. She tripped as she rushed from her chair and behind her desk to get to me. This woman, who I'd never met personally at that time, embraced me without a word and held me tight. We stayed upright, even though my legs felt as though they would collapse at any moment.

With her strong arms, she somehow held us steady. I know she gently spoke with compassion against my ear. I sobbed as I told her about our family's situation and my fathers-in-law's medical condition, probably not making much sense. When my tears were purged, I loosened my grip and she held on a few moments longer. I noticed the moist streaks on her cheeks as I backed away. *Maybe she held on longer to make sure my legs would hold me or perhaps, as I discovered later, she might have needed that hug as much as I did.*

When I left her office, the rubbery legs were gone, and I felt like a buoyant cloud. I was filled with a comfort and a confident *knowing* that all is well with my family and my soul.

This woman, who took me into her arms without a moment's hesitation, may have had her own personal adversities at the time. I learned that soon after our special hug, she left her husband, the church, and her family without any explanation.

I never saw her again to thank her. However, wherever she is, she will forever live in my heart for the unique gift of love she gave to me on that day.

The second hug came from a person who wasn't what I would call a natural-born hugger. This embrace was truly unexpected. Some people aren't comfortable with outward physical affection and I know this. I make the effort to understand and respect their

21

personal space.

I didn't know this man very well at the time. While at family gatherings, he would hang out with the men. I knew him to be uproarious with what I would call nervous energy. He had a crazy fun sense of humor. I knew this because he always seemed to create laughter in any room he occupied. I also knew he adored my very dear cousin who has always been like a sister to me. They had been married several years and, because of our busy lives, I had only seen him a few times at various family functions.

As I entered the large, empty room of the funeral home alone, my body tensed, and I wished I had waited for my husband to come home from work to accompany me. I scanned the many fresh flower arrangements lined along the outer walls and the folding chairs all in perfect rows. The soft floral scents and milieu were all too familiar throughout my life.

I checked my watch and wondered why no one was around. I then realized that I had misread the time in the obituary and had arrived early for my aunt's visitation. Since no one booted me out, I signed the guestbook and took a seat on the sofa nearest to the door—farthest from the casket. I wasn't ready to approach the reality that was across the room from me.

This was the private hour for immediate family to finalize the times and arrangements for the services, announcements, pallbearers, and any other last-minute requests. No matter how large or small your family is, with certain people, related or not, you may feel a genuine connection with some and not so much others. My connection was close and tight with this family. I knew no one would mind me being there early.

My cousin's husband paced at the opposite side of the room, appearing to be immersed in his own sorrowful thoughts, and, as far as I knew, he hadn't noticed me enter.

The beautiful woman who lay in the casket was his mother-in-law and one of my all-time-favorite aunts. I knew we both loved her deeply. I didn't know a single soul who didn't. As I squinted through my tears at the casket with blurred vision, I tried to work through my denial of who lay within the satin draping at the other end of the room.

I thought I had cried most of my tears at home in the past couple of days since the unexpected news had come. However, I felt the emotions escalate and attempted to shiver them away, along with a few deep breaths.

My cousin and I had often referred to ourselves as "the rocks" for our parents as they'd buried their parents and several brothers and sisters and other loved ones at past funerals. Since my father and my cousin's mom were the youngsters of twelve children, we'd attended many funerals before we'd become adults. Today I wanted to be that rock for my cousins, who were not only family but dear friends as well. I couldn't come close to imagining my life without my own mother. My heart was breaking for this family.

A vehement shudder ran through my body and darkness ensued. I realized I was enveloped, completely encased I imagined like a caterpillar in a cocoon would be. I felt encircled in calm. I was safe and loved and at that moment knew everything would be all right.

My cousin's husband of several years had made his way over to me and wrapped his arms around me. He rocked a bit to what seemed like soft murmurs, no words—a divine lullaby comes to mind. I can't tell you for how long he held me like that. He was a large man, and his warmth, gentleness, and the firmness of his presence were all-encompassing and unexpected.

24

The soothing comfort he brought me in those moments was from within, given by him through something so powerful, giving me strength where I had felt an immense void. I hadn't realized that the tears I had been trying to hold back had escaped and hadn't stopped since I had sat in the corner of that sofa.

By the time his wife—my cousin—returned from the office, our hug had ended. I had wiped my nose and blotted my tears. As they each greeted me, I was able to be strong like "a rock" for them—all because of that miraculous embrace that held me together from a man who was not known to speak softly or to initiate gentle hugs. I have always felt this special embrace was a Godsend for both of us to comfort and begin the grieving and healing process of the departure of this extraordinary woman in our lives.

We never spoke of this moment and now that he has transitioned also, I can only hope the retelling of this intertwined soul-touching experience speaks the truth of those moments for him, as well as myself.

The third, hug happened at my father-in-law's funeral fifteen years after his heart attacks and strokes. This hug happened after the first divine hug by the lady in the church office. For over thirty years, I've always admired the emotional, confident strength that my in-laws portray. They rarely show their emotions publicly, unlike me. I can be a blubbering mess anywhere. Whenever certain feelings hit, they tend to explode. It takes a lot of effort for me to keep any kind of control. Since I'm an emotional person, I make an extra effort to keep my composure as best I can by taking deep breaths in and exhaling slowly. I wanted to stay strong for my husband, who had done his best at being a support for his mom and our family as well through our immense sadness.

We entered the restaurant after the service and cemetery proceedings, and everyone followed the hostess to a table off to one side, separated by a peek-a-boo plank wall. The bar area positioned along the outside wall with floor-to-ceiling windows overlooking the river that could be seen through the open slats of the divider.

I happened to be the last one in as I held the door for everyone. Being a bit overwhelmed with the sadness of the day, I barely noticed the tall young gentleman off to the side taking long strides directly toward me. He lifted me off the floor, gently enfolding me in his arms. This hug felt as though heaven itself had wrapped me in a blanket of love and warmth, with a slight scent of some wonderful masculine cologne.

This young man, a tad older than my own two sons, had grown up accustomed to open affection and had always been one of those who excelled at giving loving hugs since he was able to raise his arms as a youngster. When this person hugs you, there is no doubt he cares, and he exudes the love he always feels within. On this day, this young man—my friend Faith's son—had no idea how much I needed that physical contact and what it meant to me in those moments.

Pretty soon I heard someone say, "Where's Patti," and another person answered, "Oh, there she is at the bar hugging some tall good-looking guy." My husband soon joined this unexpected reunion and he also was greeted with a hardy handshake then pulled into a hug filled with our friend's love and genuine condolences.

I realize that not everyone shares my opinion on this subject or has the same needs as I do, however there is scientific evidence of how physical contact such as hugs are pertinent to one's health and well-being. There is even a national holiday for hugs every January twenty-first, founded in 1986 to encourage people to embrace.

I recognized each of these special embraces as a spiritual divine intervention— signs, healings, and gifts sent to me at the perfect, most-needed moments.

From head to toe, there was that familiar swoosh of warmth, a confident knowing, and a tremendous comfort. I felt myself being unburdened during these hugs, tingles throughout my body, and being blanketed with that unconditional LOVE of spirit. I am so grateful.

As I reflect on the synchronicities of the who, the what, and where, my thoughts and feelings about these special interventions bring me to a place of divine knowing within myself.

It will never cease to amaze me how the Universe brings signs or people—whatever it is needed—into our lives at the perfect time when they are needed most, no matter where we are mentally, physically, or under what the circumstances.

Ponder: Have you ever had a special physical moment (hand holding, pat on the shoulder) or hug in your life that stood out as extraordinary and made you feel something more powerful that you had felt before? If so, think of the happy or sad occasion, and why do you think it was memorable?

Chapter 3

Mother Approved

"A mother's love is capable of the impossible. This love is so unconditional it can do all things." ~ P.R. Fletcher

March 2018—As I readied myself for church on Sunday, doing my ordinary routine of makeup and hair, an image of my mom came clearly into my mind. This happens often as I slather on facial lotion and think, *I'm doing it, Mom, the exact way you taught me.*

I recall the many times as a young girl that I leaned against the open bathroom door frame in my childhood home. Mom and I had some of the best chats while she moisturized and applied her make-up for the day. It never failed that she would remind me to always put lotion not only on my face but also to include the upper chest and neck, then spread it upward all the way to the top of the forehead. She'd touch wrinkles on her neck, scrunch her face and tug at the loose skin and say, "Pay attention now while you're young, because if I had done this years ago, these wouldn't be here today." And then she'd laugh.

As I smeared my all-natural rejuvenation lotion over my upper chest and all the way up to the tip of my hairline, I began to wonder what Mom would think about the church I attend now. I was raised Catholic, although my parents weren't active in the church for many years. I had made all my sacraments then stopped going for a while. Once I got married and had two miscarriages, I felt lost and like a failure. I returned to church, maybe hoping since the doctors couldn't give me any answers, maybe the church could. Unfortunately, no answers came.

After several years, I had two sons. I stayed a member of the church until my children were grown. In all those years, I watched families sit in the same pews Sunday after Sunday as their children grew and their parent's hair grayed, but I never felt a connection. I never knew the families' names and they didn't know mine, unless our children were from the same school, then we might get a friendly wave.

Sometimes I could relate to the sermons and gospels but mostly I found myself distracted and not being able to relate. However, what I always enjoyed most in church was the music and historical beauty. Church has always reminded me how powerful prayer is and to be as generous as I could be with whatever I could offer in time or service to help someone in need.

At the time when I wasn't attending any church, I'd get so wrapped up in my own family problems and personal issues that I would forget about the needs of others in the community and in the world.

It was after my parents made their transition that I became confused about death and had lots of questions. The things I thought I knew didn't make sense to me anymore. It wasn't until I began to get my answers somewhere besides the church that I finally understood. My signs, the inner knowing that came from within. The spirit within became my direct line of communication. These ethereal experiences became my truth.

It took several years before I felt the desire to return to church. The Catholic religion is all I'd ever known. However, even though I'm no longer drawn to Catholicism, I am immensely grateful for all that I have learned in the past, because it has assisted me in my spiritual growth and on my journey of understanding of who I am and why I am here today. I have a purpose and am an eternal being. I wanted to feel acceptance and like I was good enough. We are all connected with one God. I wanted to feel that.

I wasn't sure how to search for a new church, that being something I had never done. So, my plan was to choose three churches and attend each one for a month to see if I could find a good fit. I needed to feel welcome, comfortable, unjudged, and like I was meant to be there. I needed a new spiritual home, one that felt more like family and made sense to me.

I shared my dilemma with my dear friend Ella. She said, "You could try Unity. My parents attended services there before they moved and commented many times on how they felt spiritually well fed."

"Perfect," I said. "There happens to be one a few miles from my home. I'll begin my search there and see what happens after a month." Ah! I had a starting point. What a relief.

The first time I entered the local Unity church I felt an honest, glowing heartwarming welcome. Two jovial ladies opened the door to greet me. They introduced themselves and invited me to stay after church for fellowship. They said they would like to get to know me better. *Were they sincere? They seemed friendly and their smiles raised all the way up to their eyes. I hoped they wouldn't leave me alone at a table.*

I've attended Unity for several years now and I couldn't feel more welcomed, non-judged, and completely fulfilled and accepted for who I am. I feel a divine connection with the people of this church. They understand me. All of them have tried to remember my name from the first visit on. The congregation has grown in my short time there. Every week more pews are occupied. The new minister has scads of energy and fresh ideas galore. She is passionate about the church and exudes her love of Jesus through, meditation, and scripture, always making that human connection in her own wonderful, articulate, and gracious way. I felt an instant bond with her from the moment we met.

I'm not sure why, but on this particular Sunday, I wanted so badly to have a conversation with Mom about how much I loved attending this new church. I don't think we ever outgrow that childhood craving for our parent's approval. I wanted to tell her how I never dreaded going and I never wanted to leave early. I'm eager to get to church and hear the message spoken in such a touching, relatable way. I swear I feel like she picks messages for me personally. I have absolutely no anxiety conversing with the Reverend and I feel honored to spend time in fellowship with all the diverse people who attend this Unity Church. I wanted to tell Mom about each new person I've met and how each individual connection has already helped me to grow on my spiritual journey. I wanted to share with her that I've learned so much in a variety of different topics that are presented after most services. Every Sunday the scripture and sermon never fail to inspire me. It leaves me with something to ponder and relate to in my daily life, then reflect on, during the coming week. After all these years, I feel like I'm a better Christian and more spiritually connected than I've ever been in my entire life. This feeling of joy, gratitude, peace, and being connected is what I hope for all people, regardless of the religion or church they attend.

I also enjoy assisting Reverend Ana by doing announcements once a month and a reading from *The Daily Word* booklet. To speak in front of an adult group is something I'd never felt comfortable doing. Nevertheless, one day at church soon after I'd begun attending services regularly, uncontrolled words escaped from my mouth while speaking with the Reverend at the end of the service. "I'd be honored for the opportunity to be on the assist list or be a substitute for a service sometime."

Reverend Ana appeared thrilled and said, "We'll put you into the circulation next month. Thank you. You are a blessing."

As I walked away shaking my head, I thought, *where in the heck did that come from? Are you crazy? What have you done?* I took a deep breath. I had been contemplating doing something about my fear of public speaking. I guessed that this would be as good of time as any to practice and build confidence among friends before I had to speak in front of groups of strangers or do book presentations.

As I parked the car in the church parking lot, I still had Mom vivid on my mind. I wished she were alive, so I could have brought her with me today to see for herself. As I crossed the parking lot and rounded the corner to the front entrance of Unity, there on the sidewalk was an approximate three-foot perfect heart-shape, created once again from snow, only melted this time. It had dripped from the steel cross above and formed a wet area on the cement below. The point of the heart aimed toward the entrance of the church.

While I walked around the heart-shape, mesmerized, I wondered, *Is this a sign, Mom?* That familiar sensation began before the thought was even complete, the all-consuming feeling of peace, warmth, and unconditional love. It filled my body from the inside. I took a deep breath and closed my eyes. The emotions swirled as several tears slid beneath my lashes. I reached for my phone and snapped a photograph as the tender energy of my mother's love embraced me in a spiritual hug. I knew she was with me at that moment. She, without a doubt, approved of my new choice in churches. I chuckled as I thought – *no way was Mom going to be outdone by Dad's snow heart on a roof.*

When Reverend Ana asked at the end of service if there was anything anyone wanted to share, in an instant I was on my feet. I wondered, *Why?* I had absolutely no intention on sharing anything. But then I knew… It wasn't my choice. I faced this newfound congregation and tearfully shared the entire story of how much I missed my mom and that she was, without question, there with me on this day. At least forty people walked the same pathway to enter the church that morning, and not one person noticed the heart. After the service—no surprise to me—the heart I spoke of was nothing more than dry cement.

I'm eternally grateful when my signs allow me to take a photograph. Many times they disappear before I can get the picture. I haven't always understood what that message meant. Now I know that it is my permission slip or nudge from the Universe to share this miraculous personal spiritual experience with all of you. And so, it is!

This type of hug is common in our dreams, but to be fully awake and have this profound experience is one I'll treasure and remember the rest of my life. This would be what I consider my fourth spiritual hug.

Part 2 - A Miracle on a Miracle

I later heard of another even more powerful miraculous moment that came to someone else on that very day that I spoke of Mom's visit and of the melted snow heart. Several Sundays later during fellowship, Terri sat next to me. She touched my shoulder gently, and as I faced her, she closed her eyes as if to ponder something. She said, in a whisper, her expression serious, "I wasn't sure if I should share this with you or not, but then it was put on my heart to do so. It feels as if the choice isn't mine." She had my attention.

"I understand," was my response. "I've had that feeling many times over the past couple of years."

She began, "The day you spoke of your mom after service and the melted snow heart-shape out front, I had the oddest feeling come over me when you stood to speak and turned in my direction. Full body-consuming sensations swirled in my entire being. I had never in my life experienced anything that felt like that before." She shook her head slightly. "It wasn't scary. The sensation filled me with the most tender... unconditional love that I've ever felt. It was a Mother's love." Tears slid over Terri's cheeks as she continued, "I think your mom somehow used me to observe you sharing this experience with us." She kept shaking her head as if she still couldn't believe it had happened.

An instant lump formed in my throat that rendered me speechless, and my eyes filled as well. I recalled that the emotion I'd felt that day had been one of being overwhelmed, indescribably intense, and beyond my understanding. I absolutely knew with all my heart that my mother was with me that day. We both were shaking as we hugged and said our goodbyes for the week. We walked together to the door in silence with a sacred knowing that we had without-a-doubt experienced a profound miracle.

I was consumed with a genuine spiritual knowing that what Terri had explained to me was her absolute truth and yet another precious sign from God that we are never alone, that our loved ones are always near. We are all connected!

Thank you, Terri, for having the courage to share your personal experience with me and allowing me to share the experience in this book.

I have read many articles and books on angel visitations, appearing and disappearing, and wholeheartedly believe the divine intervene on our behalf, especially when asked to, however I haven't witnessed or experienced anything like this before.

Thank you, Mom, for your approval—Love You Forever and Always—Past, Present, and Future—Until we meet again. I will no longer doubt that you'll always be there for me, wherever I am and for whatever I am going through at any given time. I know you already know how this church plays such a pivotal part in my future.

Ponder: If you are not feeling spiritually filled, would you consider changing churches? Have you ever had any angel or spiritual experience like this or know of someone who has? Did you believe them? What was your response?

Chapter 4

Positive Energy and Yoga-Yuck

"How should one care for mind, body, and spirit? Begin by doing a small thing, in each category that brings joy to your heart—each day. ~ P.R. Fletcher

I had friends who'd bragged up yoga in the past. One even taught it for a while when we were in our early twenties, and she'd invited me to go many times. My thoughts were, *No thanks, I'll go to the gym or use my treadmill, like I always have.* To me yoga was stretching, I need more, and my balance has never been good. I even used the excuse of, "I have no doubt that I'd pass gas and be mortified." Anyone who has done yoga can probably relate to this very real fear.

The years zipped by and adversities presented themselves into my life, as happens to most at some point in time. Stress levels increased and I began to sink into a dark shadowy place, not knowing if there was any hope for the future. I couldn't see how things would ever get better. There would be no light without further devastation. I wasn't sure I could handle all that was upon me at that time. This made me realize how and why so many give up. I almost did more than once.

A suggestion came from a nurse at the hospital one day as I visited my father in intensive care. Every day when I showed up, Dad's medical team seemed more befuddled as to how he was still living.

One of Dad's nurses said, "Yoga is the best thing ever for stress relief. You may want to give it a try. The hospital offers classes here for your convenience." I nodded and thought, *I don't want to be at this hospital any more than I already am.* It had been almost two months. My next thought was, *Okay, what can it hurt?* Heavy sigh! When I got home from the hospital that night, I searched for a nearby place that offered beginning yoga classes. I found an advertisement for a free introductory class at a place only several blocks from my home. *Free is perfect!*

The instructor stood at the end of the colorful cubes where people stored their shoes. She was a bit taller than me with long blonde hair, and lovely straight teeth that showed with her bright smile. Her eyes reminded me of my mother's, being such an intense icy blue. She greeted everyone by name. She introduced herself to me with, "Hello, welcome. I'm Rita, are you new?"

"Yes." I chortled and said, "Warning upfront... I'm a yoga virgin."

She chuckled and said, "Not for long," and pointed me in the direction of the tiny practice room as she continued greeting the line of more-familiar faces.

Rita exuded love and compassion as she spoke about yoga and how it would encourage the new beginning of a healthier and better lifestyle. She explained how a practice of the poses could strengthen muscles and would relieve stress, among many other physical ailments.

Her warmth and sincerity radiated from across the room. Maybe it was her passion for what she was saying and doing—or maybe it was something else. There was a certain uniqueness about this person that intrigued me. I had never felt a presence this charismatic and strong.

Rita spoke in a soft tone while she instructed us to take several deep breaths. Through the next hour we heard her say, "Turn your palms upward, flex your feet, bend your knee a tiny bit more, lean into the pose. Breathe." She corrected my postures by gently using her words, fingers or her palm to apply light pressure wherever my body wasn't quite aligned properly, which turned out to be pretty much everywhere.

Over the years, my coordination and balance hadn't gotten any better. I remember thinking as I rolled out of one of the tangled-up knots, that I had never felt any sensations like this before. *Could it be the weird pose or could it be this instructor?* Her energy felt powerful. As I searched the faces around the small room, I couldn't identify anyone experiencing anything out of the ordinary.

There was no doubt I'd return, despite knowing that I didn't like yoga at all. What I did know was that I liked Rita and felt drawn to get to know her better. She fascinated me, yet I had no explanation or understanding to why or what it was about her that made me feel that way.

I still don't have it all figured out, even after several years of knowing her, and I probably never will, but I knew then, after only an hour of crazy, uncomfortable, unbalanced yoga—with no gas passed, thankfully—that we would be lifelong forever friends.

As bizarre as this may sound to some, I struggled

not to cry on the way home the first evening I attended her class. It wasn't a sad cry, just an overloaded emotional-release cry. I hadn't felt an internal peace in many months, along with gratefulness, which still happens to this day when I'm in Rita's presence. She exudes love. This person was meant to be in my life. This is an absolute knowing for me. There's a definite reason that we connected at the time we did. I believe everyone comes in our lives for a reason. Sometimes people don't stay—and that's okay. There's something they are meant to bring us or teach us while they are in our lives. Other times we are supposed to maybe teach them something. The Universe aligned and I knew I needed her in my future for unknown reasons.

Two Years Later

Rita and I met at a coffee shop one afternoon. We hadn't seen each other in quite some time because of family issues and a job change. She had heard about my book and asked several questions. She explained that she too had a dream to one day write books.

After we discussed writing, she shared in

conversation how she had felt a high positive energy radiate from me the first time we'd met at the yoga studio and thought we could be friends. My struggle with yoga that first visit had been obvious. Rita shared her fear and regret on that first day we'd met that I wouldn't ever return and she hadn't caught my name. I was a walk-in and left before I knew there was a sign-in sheet.

Rita had been wrong. I came back week after week and got better at yoga and began to understand more how the practice isn't so much about the stretches but is all about creating the meeting and connection of the mind, body, and spirit. Most importantly, this practice helped me learn to accept and love myself just as I am. I loved the way she taught and her words resonated with my heart at every session, so much that I attended her classes exclusively. Her energy never failed to comfort me in some way. It was beyond my understanding, however, I knew the energy was there. I felt it intensely, every time.

While we had coffee that day, she informed me that she had found another nearby studio to teach yoga, so I returned to a steady practice. One day after our class, she asked if I could stay afterward and chat a bit. "I would love for you to take a class with me." I had grown to enjoy and understand yoga and a tad about energy, but I had no desire to ever be an instructor. *What was she thinking?* However, I was curious and stayed.

After class, as we sat on our mats, Rita spoke of how my energy was so loving and strong that I maybe should consider taking an upcoming Reiki course with her. She was so generous and sincere that she offered to help me pay for it, if needed. She felt adamant that this was something I truly would benefit from, mentally and spiritually. "Patti, you have an extraordinary special energy gift about you. I think you would enjoy learning about it, whether you use it for anything in the future would be up to you."

It was amazing that I felt the same way about her. I don't believe in coincidences although, I believe in perfect timing.

"But I know nothing about Reiki." I said and shrugged.

"And you didn't know anything about yoga a couple of years ago and look how far you've come. Promise me you'll at least think about it?"

As promised, I thought and decided knowledge is

good. She was right. I had grown on all levels, spiritually, physically, and mentally. I called Rita to inform her that I had made my decision and to sign me up to take the Reiki one and two classes.

Rita's intuition is powerful, and she, of course, was right. I learned not just about our human energy and chakra's but so much more. There were so many facets to what I learned—things about myself, my inner being, my energy, the Universal energy, and my understanding on how energy works with all creation. I feel I've found a few more pieces to the puzzle of who I really am and why I'm here. To my surprise, the main thing I learned about was unconditional love—how to give and how to be more open to receive.

Each person's energy is as unique as the individual —changing frequently.

My experiences with Reiki have been remarkable. When someone asks me, "What is Reiki?" My answer is, even though I don't quite understand it completely, that it is the pure love energy of the Universe—God, guides, and angels—shared from a certified Reiki Master, who plays the role of a conduit for the source of healing-love energy to be transferred to the recipient. It can be hands-on or off. Rei means 'spiritual wisdom' and Ki means 'life energy.' It is a shared spiritual experience of love and healing for all involved. Nothing bad could ever come from Reiki. I have completed the second degree of studies.

There's nothing better for me to know that somehow, I can make a positive difference in someone's life or in our wonderful miraculous world, if only for few short moments at a time. It makes sense to me that if we are all connected by our creator, then why wouldn't I be able to send healing and love energies out to people, animals, even the world. Who doesn't need a little extra love? Prayer and intention are powerful.

After this certified extraordinary class experience of Reiki, I had a fleeing thought that maybe that was why Rita came into my life at the time she did, to teach me about yoga and now energy—personal, spiritually, and worldly. It made me think of the phrase that sometimes people come into our lives for a reason, season or a lifetime. I hoped there were more reasons and seasons throughout my journey. But if there aren't, I will be forever grateful for her love, friendship, and for the things Rita has taught me that have profoundly affected my life.

As it turned out, there was yet another reason for

the synchronicity of our meeting and friendship. All the while teaching yoga, Rita's intuition took her on an educational journey toward the natural healing of others, using nutrition, herbs, and homeopathies. She specializes in applied kinesiology and is presently a holistic practitioner. She has played an important role in my life thus far. She has kept me in balance, in mind, body, and spirit, even before any of my health issues arose. This has made me stronger in every area of my life. I'm so grateful for this synchronicity—this set-up of perfect timing.

Ponder: When is the last time you felt energy in a room you entered? Was it positive or negative? Have you ever felt an energy around you, maybe in the form of a powerful personality, and thought *Wow!*? If you answered yes, who came into your life and why do you think they came? Did they help you—or maybe you helped them? Are they still in your life? Either you want to get to know that person better or maybe you want to distance yourself. This feeling is our instinct, and yes, sometimes it goes beyond all understanding as to why we feel as we do.

Chapter 5

The Alarming Dream

"A smoke detectors purpose — to inform that there is smoke, fire or both and to take action to prevent further damage, or so I thought. However, I would need more snippets of this puzzle to figure out the warning." ~ P. R. Fletcher

I'm someone who hardly ever remembers my night-time adventures and rarely has had a nightmare. This is not unusual for most people. However, within the past few months, I've had two peculiar emotional and memorable dreams. The first one was about smoke detectors. You'll hear more about the second dream later.

As weird and boring as this dream may sound, it has a profound connotation for me. Once I pondered the snippet of this puzzle and figured out where the message came from and what its meaning was, it all made sense. I believe we don't have to go through life's struggles alone. We only need to recognize the signs, ponder their meaning then the knowing of who sent them and why seems to be automatic.

The Smoke-Detector Dream

Images of two smoke detectors flashed before my eyes like they had been attached to an old movie reel. They each had a tiny red light that blinked. The smoke detectors blurred then they would spin again with the images becoming more focused and moving closer to my face. They kept going around and coming back. I came fully awake, not quite shaking but certainly in somewhat of an anxious state as I sniffed the air deeply. There were no sirens, fire trucks, or plumes of smoke billowing from anywhere, nothing burning in the dream. The two detectors weren't beeping. Even though it didn't seem like an emergency, my palms were moist, my heart pounded, and my mind raced. *What is this?* I shuddered. *Could this be a warning or a message? Something deep inside told me that was exactly what it was.*

My husband had a couple days of work left before he would join me for the weekend at the lake house.

While I drank my coffee that morning, everything seemed normal. The sun's rays twinkled over the tiny ripples on the water. A hungry blue heron gulped a fish across the canal along the shoreline. The birds were all singing their summer songs. Bullfrogs were showing off their baritone call and eliciting responses from different parts of the lake. But I couldn't get my thoughts off the smoke alarms. There was one in the dining room above the table, and if I remembered correctly, we had taken the battery out at the end of the season the first year we'd owned the lake house. I stood on the dining room chair and detached the cover of the alarm. Sure enough, no battery. I couldn't remember the last time we had changed the battery in the one at home either.

Nervous energy surged through my body all that day, so much so that I texted my husband to stop on his way home from work and buy two nine-volt batteries for both of our smoke alarms. I suggested he replace the one at home that day and bring the other battery to the lake. I recounted my dream to him later that night on our evening phone call. I explained how unsettled I felt—like something was coming and that we needed to be extra careful. My husband over the years has learned to trust my intuition.

This dream was a warning or a sign, I sensed it. I knew it. *But what did it mean? A warning of what or from whom? Where was the fire going to be?* I double-checked everything at the lake house. Burners were turned all-the-way off. The oven and furnace pilot light glowed as it should. All chargers were unplugged from the outlets. The dryer vent was lint-free. The gas connections I could see all checked out. *What else can cause a fire?* I felt a bit better after these things had been marked off my list. However, that niggling sensation of something coming wouldn't subside. *I'd prefer my heart-shaped signs over this type of sign or message any day.*

As I sank into the sofa that evening, I pondered the meaning of a smoke alarm. *It is a device that lets you know there's smoke and to act immediately to lessen damage or to prevent a disaster. What disaster was coming to me and or my family?*

Several weeks went by without any mishaps or fires. I began to relax a bit and enjoyed my time at the lake house. I had no idea of what the impending dangerous situation would be. *Maybe I'd been overreacting, and it had only been a nightmare. But somehow, I knew better.* The message in my smoke detector dream would eventually reveal itself. Of that I was certain.

Ponder: Have you ever had a strong feeling that you couldn't shake? When was it? What happened? Did it happen to you or someone else? Most mothers have experienced Mother's intuition.

Chapter 6

The Promise

"Sometimes we choose a friend to be family and other times, if we're lucky, family can also become our friends!"
~ P.R. Fletcher

My cousin Amelia and I reconnected on a recent nine-hour road trip to visit our ailing uncle and one of our favorite aunts, Aunt Corrine. I had no idea that this spontaneous trip would change my life.

I have over 120 first cousins. Some I am closer to than others and some have been more like friends throughout my life. I feel it is an honor to call Amelia my dear friend and I have never quite known how to introduce her. When I say she is my cousin, it never seems like enough, then I feel moved to explain she is more of a special life-long friend than most relatives to me. Amelia is several years younger than I am and we've lived in different states most of our lives, making our visits sparse throughout the decades and making this relationship a bit more unlikely. However, whenever we have come together for a family gathering, we have always felt a strong connection.

Due to life's synchronicities, Amelia also became remarkably close friends with Faith, who I had met in high school and she had lived with our family for several years after graduation. Faith is our dear mutual friend who transitioned in 2016.

While on our road trip to Tennessee, we had a marathon of conversations about many things. We shared fun memories about our special moments with our friend Faith. We laughed. We cried. The most important part was we agreed on how grateful we were that our lives had intersected with Faith's, who was an extraordinary person in both our lives for many years.

We spoke of how Faith's friends and some of her family had been so upset that she kept her breast cancer a secret until near the end of her life. We didn't understand why, but we knew she'd had her personal reasons. Instead of a traditional funeral and wake, Faith had made the decision to have her immediate family plan a fun-filled life celebration event.

Faith knew her loved ones better than anyone else. She made the request to her family that she wanted a party, a big party with balloons and laughter, food, drinks, and music to be planned around six months after her transition.

Faith's husband and adult children would have to gather all those special items that prompted laughter and joy in Faith's life. She adored life and found beauty and joy everywhere she visited and in everyone she met. She looked for the good always.

Faith somehow knew this party-planning process would be exactly what her children and the love of her life needed to do to survive the enormous burden of grief as they mourned. They had to concentrate on gathering all her collected treasures, foods, names of the places she'd visited, and the fun events that had brought Faith so much joy while she'd lived. They would have to somehow incorporate them into the celebration. By doing this, they'd bring forth their own memories of her laughter and love through the years as they remembered how excited she'd get when she found a new snowman for her ever-growing collection, how her nose scrunched and her eyes twinkled as she sniffed her favorite perfume and candle scents, how she'd danced to her favorite Bob Seger songs, the bargains she'd found as she shopped at the stores she loved or visited those take-your-breath-away places, and how she delighted in so many foods, desserts, and a great cup of coffee. They had plenty of stuff to go through before this celebration could take place.

Through the months of planning, the family took their time and listened to people share their loving, up-lifting, and fun experiences of how Faith had touched each of their lives in her generous, compassionate ways.

There were also tons of family photos and movies to go through to bring all those memories together for this special gathering.

The hundreds who attended will never ever forget Faith, her unique life celebration party, and especially her way of showing love to everyone she met. She touched many lives, and I have absolutely no doubt that she continues to do so in her heavenly body.

Mine and Amelia's road trip to visit our aunt and

uncle in Tennessee was one to be remembered. Somehow, Amelia and I managed to chat and share for over nine hours one way and again on the way home three days later. I think we both needed this type of deep, honest communication from the heart and soul to help each other heal.

Our conversations returned to our early childhoods, our parents—mothers who were close sisters and all their silly sibling shenanigans—our immediate family's adversities and their accomplishments. However, it didn't take long, and we would return to some topic or memory that involved our dear friend Faith.

Here is part of one of our many conversations in the car that day.

"Did Faith go for regular mammograms?" Amelia asked in her soft voice.

"No one said," I replied, "and no one asked, to my knowledge."

"And, when was your last mammogram?" Amelia

suddenly demanded in a voice I hardly recognized from her usual mellow tone.

I shrugged and said, "Um, probably a year ago, maybe two. I'm overdue. Time slips away quickly."

"You have to promise me right now that when we return, you will make an appointment. Please, promise me!" Amelia said in her normal voice.

I nodded as I drove. I had read a few articles on the pros and cons about mammography and hadn't made up my mind about it one way or another. I didn't bring this up. I'm a naturalist and don't like the idea of any kind of radiation near or on my body. The more I had read on the controversy of an annual mammogram and how they are not always conclusive made me wonder… *With all that you must go through, is the procedure necessary?*

Amelia wasn't happy with only a nod. "Say it out loud." she demanded twice, like barking an order. "Say it. 'I promise to make my mammogram appointment as soon as I get home.'" She insisted I repeat the words to her, so, I did. Most people who know me personally know I don't break promises— and I didn't break this one either.

I decided to have this mammogram done at a

different facility than I'd previously used, one that wasn't so far away. The radiologist from my former office agreed to send all my past films from the previous years to the new location. As promised, I made the earliest appointment available once I returned home. The mammogram would be done three weeks from the day I called.

At the clinic, as I sat across from the mammography technician, she went over my paperwork and verified all the information. She asked, "Are you aware that it has been four years since your last mammogram?"

"Four years! There must be some mistake. Are you sure?" I asked. I'd told Amelia I was a little overdue, but not four years. I hadn't realized so much time had passed.

She nodded and pointed to the last file date. "Have you heard about the newer 3D mammography machine?"

I shook my head and shrugged. She explained how the machine experience was the same, but the images are sharper and went deeper into the dense tissues. "However," she said, as her voice lowered, "insurance companies don't always cover the cost of this newer technology and some will only pay a percentage. It's a darn shame."

I was still in a stupor that so much time had escaped me. "Okay," I said instantly. "I'll try out your new machine since it's been so long. I'll pay the extra charges if they occur."

In my life, I've been called 'Ms. Coupon Clipper.' I'm a bargain finder along with being a dedicated clearance shopper. It's highly unusual for me to volunteer for an extra expense, knowing that my insurance would cover the cost of a regular mammogram. The other thing is that my husband and I have always discussed where our money was being spent before we made our decisions. Usually, I would do my own research on this new machine before agreeing to any procedure or test.

Everything about this snap decision seemed out of character for me. However, it turned out to be instinct of the purest kind. I'd just known in that moment what I needed to do.

So, because of this spontaneous road trip with my

dear, sweet cousin and special friend, Amelia, I believe the rest of my allotted time here on earth will be healthy and treasured even more. If I would not have promised to have that mammogram, I'm certain I would have put it off once again, time would have sped by, and most likely the growth that they discovered would have become even more troublesome and possibly it would have been too late to do anything about. Mere words can't express my gratefulness.

Amelia is a loving, kind, honest, generous soft-spoken person and I know her honest heart and mind will always show Amelia her life's purpose, even if it means being a bit demanding to a cousin. I'm so honored to be a part of this time and space and have this lifetime special connection with her.

I don't believe it was luck for even a nano-second. I'm positive there were several synchronicities involved.

I feel in my soul that Faith, our mutual girlfriend, was determined to get me to the doctors for that mammogram and she voiced this through Amelia with an 'I'm not taking no for an answer'-type attitude and firm voice with which Faith was known for on occasion, but not Amelia—At least not with me, ever. What a priceless gift I had received!

PONDER: Have you ever wondered why maybe you have been prompted by someone else's adamant suggestion or idea? Has anyone spoke to you in a way that was completely out of character to their personality about a subject or problem you may have in your life, whether they knew about the situation or not? Was there a message? Did you listen? Have you thought after you said something to someone else, *I can't believe I said that!* or *Where did that come from?*

Chapter 7

The First Procedure

"I believe, accept, and am grateful for the comfort and unconditional love of my deceased loved ones." ~ P.R. Fletcher

Near the end of summer, I received a call to have that *promised* mammogram repeated due to a suspicious growth in an area on the image that wasn't on any of my previous films. I've had them redone before and the results had always come back fine. This time, as much as I tried to remain positive, negative thoughts inched their way into my mind. I somehow knew the end results wouldn't match my previous ones, with the results always being, "You're fine. It's just dense tissue. We'll see you next year."

Once they'd repeated the mammogram, they decided to do an ultrasound. From here the doctor who read both reports recommended a biopsy, a procedure done as an out-patient in a clinic within the hospital. At this point, I realized I hadn't been in a hospital since my children had been born over three decades ago.

In my previous book I spoke of being an only child and the amazing relationship I had with my parents, always. I feel our closeness continues, even though they have transitioned. We still have a special unconditional love connection. They have comforted me on occasion using several different signs, though it's mostly hearts that I connect with them. Knowing I'm never alone is one of the most powerful things that keeps me strong and gives me daily hope, trust, and positivity.

During the procedure of the biopsy, I sensed both Faith's and my mom's presence. The doctor didn't drug me, only numbed the area. They said I could watch the ultrasound monitor if I desired, to see the entire procedure of the wire and a minuscule metal clip insertion to instruct the surgeon—if surgery was needed—to the exact area of the tumor. I didn't. I closed my eyes and tried to block out the communication between the doctor and the nurse.

I attempted to meditate while lying in an uncomfortable position on the hard table. Their voices and words turned into murmurs. The stillness didn't happen as it usually does at home during a meditation practice, and I felt a tear slid down my cheek. The moment I became aware of the tear—it was within seconds—I felt the calm presence of unconditional love surrounding me and the fear dissipated, immediately. I knew I wasn't alone with these strangers in this cold, sterile room any longer. Ever so softly, I felt two hands cup my face, palms on my chin. I clearly heard my mother's whisper, "There's nothing to fear. It's going to be all right. Trust me." Next to Mom was the perfect shadowed image of my dear friend Faith. She tilted her head a bit and gave me her best sort of crooked grin, along with that familiar sparkle and confidence that could always be seen in her eyes. My body felt warm with tingles. When I opened my eyes, I realized there was a wide smile on my face. I heard the doctor say, "That'll do it. You're done. You seemed so calm and grinned through the entire procedure. Wow! Great job!"

If there is anything that can test a person's faith and positivity, it is the possible diagnosis of any disease. And when that diagnosis contains the word 'cancer', one knows life will never be the same.

They put several thin white tape strips on the insertion area and sent me home to wait a few days until the results came back. Even after I had received so many absolute signs, for over a decade, I still asked, *Did that just happen? Did I imagine Mom and Faith with me during the biopsy?* When these doubts come about—and they do on occasion—I always request another sign to validate what I felt or envisioned, because sometimes it seems so unbelievable. This was one of those times. I asked for a validation but didn't receive any answers right away.

It wasn't until the next morning as I dressed that I noticed a dark marbled mark beneath my arm. It was a bruise, and I wouldn't have paid any attention except it was set apart from the incision area and tape. The bruise formed a lovely butterfly image. I traced the edges gently with my finger; it was one in flight with four wings spread wide. I immediately burst into tears and knew with that inner knowing that it was my confirmation sign from Faith. Here's why…

Faith's Butterfly

The day my friend Faith made her transition, there was a perfect in-flight-shaped butterfly cloud outside her building. I noticed it but didn't pay much attention as I continued to search the sky for a heart sign from

Mom and Dad, as they'd loved Faith too, and I was sure they were near to greet her. Later that day, I discovered that Faith adored butterflies and had for many years, a subject I guess we'd never talked about. I didn't know. Since that day, butterflies have always brought my thoughts to Faith.

There it was, my sign that she was with me and, in that moment, I knew she would be by my side to help me through whatever came next—and along the entire journey. Gratitude was all I felt.

The morning following Faith's sign, the same thing happened, only this time the butterfly bruise had made a complete transformation into a perfect marbled heart-shape. Once again, the tears flowed, and I felt extraordinarily blessed and overwhelmed with gratitude for my life and all the love I have found throughout and within. I was confident that whatever the biopsy results were, I was loved unconditionally by both the living and my transitioned loved ones, and I was absolutely, positively, never alone. What great hope they gave me.

Mom transitioned in 2010 and my dear friend Faith left this world in 2016 with stage four breast cancer after only six months of being diagnosed. They both have appeared to me at my scariest moments.

The comfort and confidence they have swaddled me in, has in fact kept me from diving into that place of darkness.

Ponder: Have you ever been blanketed in an unexplainable calm or an all-consuming peace? What was going on in your life at the time? What did you feel or think after the calm came? Did someone you love or that loves you unconditionally find their way into your thoughts, living or deceased?

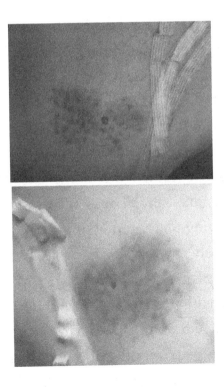

Chapter **8**

Ella's Surprise Visit

Synchronicities

"I'm always in the right place at the right time—I have human and divine guidance without even asking. I'm unconditionally loved and am never alone." ~ P.R. Fletcher

I was later told how lucky I had been after the 3D mammogram revealed a tiny tumor that a regular mammogram probably would not have shown, since that tiny mass was buried so far beneath dense tissue.

I didn't want this sequel to be another cancer book, however, it was put on my heart to write about all the love, extraordinary signs, and messages I've received connected with this part of my life's journey. There have been so many miracles to celebrate!

When Ella asked if she could come for a visit, my answer was an instant, "YES, I miss you like crazy. It's been forever." It took about two seconds for that excitement to diminish and for me to become a bit anxious.

It had only been a few days since I had spoken with the doctor about the biopsy results. The tumor was cancerous, though at this point we didn't know to what extent. No one knew except my immediate family. I had been inundated with information and was trying to wrap my head around the fact that I had breast cancer. My moods had been a bit chaotic the past few days and I felt like I was trapped in a heavy gray fog. Mentally it was the first time I realized that my life was about to change or possibly end abruptly. *It might not be the best time for a visit, but I sure could use some of Ella's fun, uplifting encouraging, unconditional loving personality.*

We had spent nearly every weekend doing fun things until she'd moved thousands of miles away a few years ago. Even with the distance, we've always found a way to get together once or twice a year. We have that special connection where it doesn't matter how much time goes by. We can always pick up right where we left off.

"The visit will take your mind off things," my husband said, "Tell her to come."

I knew I would share my diagnosis with her, but it could wait until later when I found out more details. I knew Ella needed a bit of downtime also. She had been extra busy with all that she had on her own plate, which included all wonderful things like new a newfound romance, grand-babies, her daughter's engagement, wedding plans, travel, and her youngest son, who is an airman, changing locations. I didn't want to add an extra serving to her dish, especially one of sadness—a helping of, 'My best friend has breast cancer.'

My intentions were to allow time for Ella to chat about all the fabulous things that had been going on in her life. I wanted to hear all about everything and everyone. I would get around to telling her my news eventually. *Maybe I'd tell her on the ride back to the airport when she was leaving, and our fun week together had ended.* Through the decades we'd been friends, I'd shared everything with her, more like a sister. All I had at this time was the diagnosis from the biopsy, along with the many unknowns. They wouldn't be able to determine what kind of treatments or how many until after I had the lumpectomy. Those results would tell if the cancer had spread.

The Universe was once again in control. Ella arrived around two in the morning. She gave me one of her fabulous *love-you* hugs as she wheeled her luggage to the guest room and said, "I'm exhausted. We can talk in the morning when we are refreshed. You know if we get started, we'll be up all night." She was right. It had happened many times before. I was tired and had had a long day. Even though I was excited to see her, I felt grateful to go to bed.

First thing in the morning, I received another wonderful hug and she began to tell me about her flight as I made coffee. "I was so embarrassed that everyone on the plane kept looking at me. I couldn't stop the tears. The special feature on the monitor had been a documentary about children with cancer. Some survived and others didn't. I can't even imagine why I watched it." She grabbed a tissue.

This was not our normal opening conversation, especially before breakfast. We hadn't even asked about each other's families yet, which in the past has always been our first topic. I sensed our connection being off. Our energy felt odd.

Our conversation eventually progressed to how everyone in our families had been doing. And after breakfast, we decided to take a short road trip to the lake house for a few days.

Once there, we enjoyed the outdoors by taking a walk around the lake. We both love to be near water and in nature. Gathering wood for an early campfire, Ella told me how our mutual friend Faith—who we'd both met her in high school and all graduated together—had been heavy on her mind lately, probably because of their shared love of babies. I nodded and said, "She's been on mine too, more than anyone knows." I didn't mention my reason being quite so different from hers. Ella seemed to think that our deceased friend Faith was on her mind because of the recent arrival of her first grandchildren, identical twin girls. I'm sure this was partially true, but I believe and know in my heart that Faith had another reason.

As our conversation continued, she brought up the question about whether Faith had ever had mammograms. I assume that question had crossed all our minds since she'd died of stage four breast cancer. I said, "I don't know."

"I don't understand why Faith kept her illness a

secret until near the end of her life." Ella said, "It just doesn't make sense to me."

"Those were her choices to make," I said, softly. Of course, I now understand a bit better. It's difficult to talk about any disease, let alone a cancer diagnosis. People feel heartsick when you tell them, then they ask lots of questions or make friendly suggestions when you are already thoroughly overwhelmed. Some even treat you differently or shy away from your company or communication completely. It's a conversation that affects everyone around you, and Faith had always been an optimistic, positive, fun-loving person and likely wanted to remain so without the subject of cancer being the dominant topic of every conversation when friends and family visited. I was beginning to understand.

The very next subject Ella brought up went into more conversation about mammograms and wondering if they do more harm than good. Ella likes to research things as much as I do. She mentioned an article she had read. It spoke of the arguments on the newer 3D Mammogram verses the regular Mammography machines. She added, "My insurance doesn't cover the new technology."

I immediately said, "Mine doesn't either. I had the 3D one a month ago. I'd highly recommend going with the newer technology anyway, especially if you've been told you have dense tissue."

Since cancer in some form or another had been brought up so many times in the few hours we'd been together, I decided to take that as my sign. It was time to share the diagnosis with her, even though it was only our first whole day together. I couldn't hide the emotions or frustrations any longer if she was going to keep talking about cancer.

Of the many friends that have impacted my life, Ella has a special place in my heart and by many has been considered 'Ms. Positivity and Encouragement.' Those characteristics have always been the basis of her life's purpose as far as I could tell. It was those strengths I needed at this exact time in my life in these staggering moments of uncertainty, whether I wanted to admit it or not. Since we were teenagers, we have always been there for each other through all our life's adversities and amazing celebrations.

I sensed with all my being that our mutual friend Faith was heavy on Ella's mind, not only because of those adorable babies but also because Faith knew I needed some extensive encouragement from one of the best people I knew in the whole world. I had no idea what was going to happen next or how far along my cancer was at this point. Once again, perfect timing...Somehow after I told her what was happening, we managed to have lots of laughs through the week and kept the cancer talk to a minimum.

Ponder: Has anyone ever called or come over at the exact time you had thought of them or you needed to vent or share other news? Or have you been nudged to call someone or visit when it was unplanned or to say something you had no idea you were going say? How did you feel when they left—or when you left them?

Chapter 9

World Day of Prayer—And a Special Surprise

"Things may happen around you, and things may happen to you, but the only things that matter are the things that happen in you." ~ Eric Butterworth

Ella's departure date happened to be on the same day my church would be celebrating its 25th World Day of Prayer service. The airport is close to my winter home and church. This made it possible for me to attend the service for the first time. It's always held on the second Thursday of September and carries a different International theme every year. Some of the past topics were, *Pray Up Your Life* in 2015 and in 2019 it was *Infinite Presence, Unlimited Potential.* I have missed all of these special services because I stay at the lake house from May until the end of October.

World Prayer Day, Evening

I loved seeing everyone since I had been absent since May. I miss my spiritual family through the summer months, although there is rarely a day that goes by that I don't think about and pray for each of them. I'm grateful for their love and understanding the whole year.

To begin the evening, each person was handed a program. On every chair there was a thin cardboard package that contained a compact disk. Reverend Ana is so generous, always giving us that inspiring bit of something extra. I wondered if someone in our church had created this special CD, assuming it was a musical one.

My jaw dropped in disbelief when I read the title *"Prepare to Be Healed— Meditations for Before and After Medical Treatments."* My eyes filled—knowing this was not a coincidence. I had only shared my diagnosis with four people and not with anyone at my church yet. I could only shake my head, knowing that the synchronicity of life had shown up once again with perfect timing.

The service encompassed an incredible number of

tools for healing each of us, our loved ones, our country, and our entire world. Several Bible verses were read by Reverend Ana and a few of our members sang. One of our indigenous ladies, Sherry played the drum as she chanted a healing prayer. Saroja's choice of songs and voice sung from the depth of her soul had tears streaming over my cheeks. My friend Kay played a sacred singing bowl. I felt the vibrations swirl within my being like a bright cyclone, the white light of healing. How unique and special it was to have all this diversity within one service.

In our church, my dear friend Jeanie is the person who coordinates and organizes this extraordinary service, plus many others. She read one of the most inspiring stories I have ever heard—the story of: Evy McDonald from the book, "Quest for Wholeness," by Robert Brumet.

Once I returned home, my husband asked how the service had gone, I burst into emotional tears. I told him that the experience was like nothing I had ever felt before. Everything about the entire evening stirred something deep within me. I felt the vibrational power of the healing prayers and moved forward with a renewed confidence and positivity about my upcoming surgery. There was no doubt I was being taken care of and that I wasn't fighting this battle alone. The healing had already begun.

I'm so grateful for Jeanie. It was her smile and kindness that first welcomed me through the doors of Unity Church several years before. I'm especially honored to be a part of her life and of the many fabulous events that she plans. Her generosity and unconditional love for the church, its congregation, and humankind goes above and beyond. This service deeply touched not only me, but the entire human race. Yes, I believe our intentions and prayers go that far.

This Unity Church service came at the perfect time for me. I need never underestimate God's timing and His way of supporting me through this human journey and dis-ease. I'm so thankful He uses Jeanie and Reverend Ana as a conduit for His messages and makes sure I'm exactly where I need to be, all in perfect timing.

The rhythm of Sherry's drum and the lovely vibrations of the sacred singing bowl as Kay prayed were aimed directly at me. And Saroja? Oh my, she is gifted with love, words, and a voice that seems to resonate clarity and peace through the mind, body, and soul. I felt as though I was wrapped in a holy healing bubble that glowed all the way home.

The readings were perfect. The songs flowed through me and touched my spirit. The story Jeanie shared brought tears and reiterated how we must love ourselves and see this wondrous love through God's eyes, not focus on how we feel we are flawed. I felt the strong presence of unconditional Love and Truth that evening, and I have no doubt every person, state, and group we prayed for aloud and within our hearts felt our combined prayers of comfort, unconditional love and healing, along with God's.

I believe all that Jeanie has done makes a miraculous difference to every life she has encountered. She does it with a glowing genuine love that seems to overflow from every pore.

Jeanie's words, her friendship, and her love has impacted me greatly and has indeed changed my life. Thank you, Jeanie, for all your time, efforts, and energy—and especially for sharing your light and love with the world.

Ponder: Can you think of a time spontaneous tears sprang to your eyes? Where were you and why did that happen? Has something touched you within so profoundly, to the point of reaching your soul? What was it you felt? When did it happen and why do you think it happened? Did you learn something from the experience? Where were you and what brought you to that place?

Chapter **10**

Prepared to be Healed

"We can become bitter or better as a result of our experiences."
~ Eric Butterworth

The CD, "Prepare to Be Healed", is phenomenal. My confidence and faith grew a bit more each time I listened to the meditation. I played it as much as possible, at least once or twice a day before my surgery. One of the scripture readings on the CD, read by Reverend Moran is, Jeremiah 30:17. Throughout the guided meditation experience, he repeats God's promise: "I will restore health to you and your wounds I will heal." What conquerable words. The clarity came in an instant. Every time I was hurt, sick, cut, bruised, hadn't I healed? Reverend Moran's voice soothed and made me realize I once again was in the presence of a miracle and needed to trust.

This CD by Reverend Moran has another part that spoke specifically to my soul. It's selfish maybe, but I felt this next verse was connected directly to my

.dical team and meant for me to hear. He began in his almost-hypnotic voice and spoke the words from Isaiah 42:16, "Paths they have not known I will guide them and will turn the darkness before them into light and rough places into level ground. These are the things I will do, and I will not forsake them."

The doctor, moments before doing the biopsy, had pointed out my tumor on the monitor. I saw light, smooth areas along with some high and low spots of gray, however it was the darkened place his finger landed on that stood like a raised black hill and caused me to gasp as I remembered the words in the meditation. At that point, all I wanted was for that dark place to be light and level again. I felt all alone in those seconds right before the procedure—until I wasn't...

I didn't need to doubt or even know why. I had only to remember to trust that the people, prayers and even CD's would show up in my life with His perfect timing and guidance when needed.

I could not have been more comforted by any person more than the words on this recording during my pre-surgery days. This CD is profound and powerful. I felt a divine intervention whenever I meditated with Reverend Moran.

Each time the meditation ended, my body felt like a childhood rag-doll, limp, relaxed, comforted, and loved unconditionally. I recommend this CD to anyone who must go through or is anxious about their medical procedures. At the time, I had no doubt that side two, "After Medical Procedure and Treatments" would be just as much or more of a blessing as side one.

I'm confident that the nudge that Reverend Ana received to purchase that CD for the World Day of Prayer healing service probably came for several reasons. That tiny voice inside that she speaks of often in her sermons told me that I was one of those reasons.

It is more than coincidence that the CD showed up in my life when I had only been diagnosed a couple of weeks prior to the service. At that time I also had no intention of attending that special service, knowing I would be up north at the lake house. My mind and heart were on an emotional rollercoaster with not knowing what was around the next curve.

Thank you, Reverend Ana, for being His conduit, as always, to bring about these extraordinary powerful programs with their miraculous messages and the ideal gifts to distribute to everyone in the congregation. You are phenomenal!

Synchronicity and the Universe proved once again that I had been nudged to be in the perfect place at the perfect time. Everything aligned. I'm grateful I listened.

May your bright light and unconditional love continue to flow into Unity Church, its members, and the world.

Ponder: Through the years of your life, who has impacted and influenced your spiritual journey the most, and why? In hindsight, can you see the synchronicity's? How did you react? What extraordinary moments do you remember?

Chapter 11

The Superpower of a Mother's Love

"Mom's sense of humor came through loud and clear."
~ P.R. Fletcher

After I received the results from the biopsy—stage one breast cancer. I did the best I could to keep my chin up and thought about all the people suffering with worse diseases or situations than mine. I remembered all my friends and relatives through the years who have struggled with some sort of pain or disability in their everyday life—even my own parents and how the medical field had helped them. I put on my positive attitude hat and felt relaxed and grateful that I would have choices, and I wondered what decisions I would have to make in the future.

The doctors highly recommended a lumpectomy to find out if the cancer had traveled into the lymph nodes or anywhere else.

My treatments would then be determined by the lab results of the tumor, nodes, and surrounding cells that the surgeon would remove. The next step was to meet with the surgeon and the oncology team so they could explain to my husband and me what to expect in the coming weeks after the surgery and to go over the detailed report from the biopsy. Things, of course, could change, depending on the lumpectomy results.

My husband and I would be scheduled to attend a four-hour consultation into the world of cancer. The nurse handed me a large pink goodie bag filled with a three-ring binder, pamphlets, books, appointments sheets, and business cards for all the different doctors and nurses, along with a few comfort items. It was official, I was now on the cancer patient list and my goal was to get to the other list—the survivor list. The nurse escorted us to a tiny room to wait for the surgeon to discuss possible ifs and options. In those moments I felt bombarded and overwhelmed, mentally and physically. It seemed time had stopped. The reality of having cancer seeped in and I knew this was only the beginning.

A soft knock on the door interrupted my thoughts before the surgeon entered. My shoulders were slumped, my gaze toward the floor. Within seconds, I laughed a bit too loudly, probably nerves, however I had noticed the surgeon had on super-cute shoes and I told her so. They were shiny black clog-like ones with bright colors, flowers and insects—believe it or not butterflies and dragonflies. I love both species. They were not the kind of shoes one would expect a surgeon to wear, at least in my mind. They made me smile as I raised my eyes to meet hers. She chuckled and said, "I stole them from my mother's closet. They were so comfortable I had to have them." Laughter is always a good way to begin a serious conversation.

She explained the pages of statistics, graphs, and numbers that were on the results of the biopsy report then the standard options for this type of cancer. They, of course, would know more about what kind of treatments and how many would be needed after the results came back from the lumpectomy. She said, "It's most likely your cancer will be treated with radiation to prevent it from returning in the same area, if it has spread, you may also have to have chemotherapy treatments."

I didn't like either choice but had more research to do to see if there were any natural options available.

I had a routine vital check before we were led into a different room with a television to watch specific short video clips, showing different surgeons and available medical help. The television played while my husband and I sat holding hands, sort of in a daze. Periodically the nurse would come in and say, "Oh wait, you don't have to watch this one." She'd click to the next one. The videos showed different doctors on the hospital team as they explained the whys and hows of what they specialize in, ranging from reconstructive surgery to different physical and mental therapies. It was all so depressing, even though each presentation was well done with a compassionate doctor.

After what felt like ten hours of trying to pay attention, I lost interest. My head felt heavy and ready to explode. My shoulders drooped lower. I felt lost, alone, and defeated, without any control of what was happening or about to happen in my life at that moment. I imagined my husband was feeling the same.

I laid my head on his shoulder and closed my eyes. Just as I did, a loud uplifting voice came from the video that was playing. This female doctor on the monitor cheerfully introduced herself using—I still can't believe this—*my mother's full name.* I straightened and slowly raised my eyes, expecting to actually see my mother standing there in the room with us—or at least see her face on the monitor. "Did you hear that? Did she say what I think she said?" I asked my husband. He nodded as his eyes glassed over. According to him, I guess I sort of lost it then. What began as nervous laughter shortly turned into sobs. I hadn't cried—only teared up here and there—or felt the need to, since this rollercoaster had begun over two months before. I was determined to remain my usual positive self. I would find the good in all of this. No matter how difficult it was, I knew the puzzle pieces would come together for my highest good or for the highest good of all concerned.

These tears from hearing my mother's name spoken in such a confident, cheerful way were torrential; however, they were not sad tears. Hearing her name was exactly what I needed to hear to carry on—a reminder of her optimism. After a few seconds, the nurse came in and said, while handing me more tissues, "Oh, I'm so sorry that this video has upset you. It wasn't even one you needed to watch." She had no idea; it was truly the only one I'd needed to watch and to hear.

The knowing beyond all understanding came the next few seconds my mother was with me in that office in that moment. I felt her positivity, comfort, encouragement and saw her always a bit tilted, humorous grin. I loved her sign and message. She has always been a practical joker and full of surprises. I guess some things never change. Mom as a surgeon was hilarious. Good one, Mom!

The surgeon returned to the room to answer any questions we might have had about the videos and to discuss radiation. She said, "Imagine the sun and its powerful rays disintegrating any left-behind cancer cells. The radiation unfortunately kills the healthy cells also, but they can and will reproduce. The cancer cells are destroyed and never return in that area."

I had no trouble making the decision to have the extra mammograms, ultrasounds, biopsy, and even the lumpectomy, but the idea of radiation disturbed me. With all the above, why was this decision so difficult for me?

I struggled with the radiation decision mentally, physically, and spiritually. I shared my preferred holistic beliefs with the medical team. I expected them to be upset with me or somehow discredit my thoughts. I've treated most every ailment in my life with natural remedies, switching household items to green, eating organics, and using only chemically clean toiletries. I've worked hard to lessen the amounts of radiation in my life by giving up the usage of a microwave many years ago and only having one x-ray per year at the dentist, despite his urging me to have more. I never have kept my cell phone on my body or in the bedroom and I had considered limiting my mammograms to every other year. I'd totally blown that last one.

Lumpectomy Results

The lab reports after the lumpectomy confirmed stage one cancer fed by the estrogen in my body, the great news being the cancer had not traveled to the nodes or anywhere else. The surgeon said she felt she had removed the mass and much of the surrounding tissues, which all looked healthy, and confidently told me she believed that she had gotten it all. I felt with all my being that she had. I didn't understand this big push for me to undergo treatments. I guess it's just a protocol for extra protection.

The oncology team consulted, agreed, and recommended that I should have twenty treatments of radiation. It was decided that chemotherapy was not needed at this time. I was grateful for one less decision to make, since I hadn't yet made up my mind about the radiation. The hospital set up an introduction orientation appointment with the radiologist and his staff so I could receive detailed information surrounding the treatments and what to expect before I made my decision.

I knew in my heart I didn't want to have any treatments. Everything about it went against what I felt and believed. I had made all those efforts to avoid radiation and now they wanted to blast it into my body. Just when I thought I had made up my mind not to have the treatments, I wondered, *Could the fire detector dream's message be about finding this cancer early, before it could spread, or was it about having the radiation treatments, burning away maybe hidden cancer cells that were possibly there—or both? Universe, please give me another snippet to this puzzle.*

That confident knowing with the mental and physical sensations that I usually get with intense messages still hadn't presented themselves as clearly as I would have liked, especially when it was explained to me that radiation doesn't actually burn the skin, even though it feels and appears to be burnt. I was told that is a misnomer.

Ponder: Have you ever heard the name of a deceased loved one on the radio or television or over a store intercom? Or, maybe you saw a billboard or magazine cover with the familiar name? How did it make you feel? Was there some adversity happening at the time in your life? Did you need encouragement? Did you feel alone? Have you seen someone while in a grocery store or somewhere else that their appearance seemed exactly like someone you knew who had passed on?

Chapter 12

My Nemesis

". . . In spite of Virtue and the Muse,
Nemesis will have her dues,
And all our struggles and our toils
Tighter wind the giant coils." ~ Ralph Waldo Emerson

My initial appointment with the radiologist was prefaced by some paperwork and a nurse who came in to take my vitals. She explained how the treatments would be done if I chose this preventative care. I admit that my attitude was petulant. Usually, I try to control my facial expression if I disagree with someone, especially a professional. Not this day... I didn't want to be there; I didn't want them putting radiation in my body. I didn't like anything this nurse had to say. She didn't even have on super-cute shoes. I wanted a natural alternative and they offered none.

I was told that this was the best the medical field had to offer at this time and that fact was backed up by tons of research and statistics. The overly cheerful nurse persisted in telling me how lucky I was to have this treatment at my disposal, because years ago, I would have needed a complete mastectomy, not a partial. They gave me a quick tour of the rooms where the radiation was administered and instructions of what I needed to do each day that I had a treatment. If I decided soon, my treatments would be done before Christmas. Before we left the building, my name was on the schedule and I would receive my three permanent tattoos—markings for the area to radiate— the following Monday. My tattoos weren't colorful, pretty, or of any character or fancy artistic design. They were merely dots. However, they represented a path along my life's journey that would never be forgotten.

None of this information or the statistics made me feel any better. When my husband and I had left that day, I snarled as I held back the tears, and said, "That nurse reminds me of a sleazy used-car salesman, only trying to sell me radiation. I didn't like it one bit, and from that point I referred to her as my nemesis.

Now, to be honest as I reflect back, I believe she made me one of her weekly challenges and put a noticeable amount of positive effort, energy, and kindness into convincing me that I had made the right decision. Even on the days she wasn't my nurse, she would poke her head in my room and inquire about how I was doing that day. On my third or fourth visit, with my disposition still not in a good place, she said something I hadn't thought about to help me cope a tiny bit better. My nemesis knew what was bothering me. I had explained that I was a naturalist and felt this treatment to be a horrible four-week invasion of my body and that radiation was something I had tried to avoid for decades. She sighed and said, "You know, radiation does come from the earth, if that helps any. Multitudes of people are grateful to these scientists and doctors who discovered this method that kills specific cancer cells in the distinct areas of their bodies—and has lengthened their lives." This is the conversation that somehow began the shift in my thinking. I knew many people who were grateful for this treatment and survived way worse cancers than I had, I would get through this and I would work on my pissy attitude and be more grateful.

About halfway into my treatments, she had earned my respect, but it was still fun for me to refer to her as my nemesis, mostly to my husband. It made me grin and made him laugh, seeing he is a big fan of Phineas and Ferb, a cartoon that is based on a friendly nemesis. Believe me... Anything that brings on laughter during these times is a treasure—even at her expense. Sorry, Nurse Chloe!

On the day of my final treatment, I had heard from the front desk at check-in that my nemesis wanted to talk to me before I left the building. While I was laying beneath the green laser lights for the last treatment, the radiation therapist reminded me again that the nurse wanted to speak with me before I left. *I couldn't imagine why. I had hoped she hadn't heard me call her a nemesis.*

To my astonishment it had nothing to with name-calling but the total opposite. She had read my book, *This Sign Was Mine. Message Received!* and it touched her heart to the point of tears. She could barely get the words to form over the lump in her throat as she told me this.

It turned out my nemesis and I have many personality traits and interests in common, and several things in my book touched her soul. She thanked me for writing the book that was so relatable to her own life and held out her arms for an extra-long embrace. I was drawn to her like a magnet. I was blown away, to say the least, and tears filled my eyes as well. The hug that day was filled with something beyond special. It was ethereal love. I felt the gossamer wings of an angel surround me. I knew I had done the right thing. This was my fifth spiritual hug. If this keeps up, I'll have to write another book just on hugs. *Not really.*

Ponder: Have you ever met someone and instantly didn't like them? Why? Did that first impression ever change? Why? Did things turn out differently than you thought?

Chapter 13

Faith Shows Up...in More Ways Than One

"Butterflies . . . Flowers that fly, and all but sing."
~ Robert Frost

I believe that the dream about the smoke detectors was a definite sign from my departed friend Faith. The reason this makes sense to me is because, as a child, Faith was severely burned and extremely self-conscience of her scars. We had talked about her fear of fire many times.

And to add to my story of that dream...

We do one home improvement per season at the lake house to keep it updated. This year it was decided that our central air unit was making so much noise that it not only disturbed us but also our surrounding neighbors as well. It had gotten more obnoxious each passing year. We don't use it often or it would have been gone a while ago.

At the time we noticed the loudness, the air was working fine. We'd called a professional out several years ago to look at it so hopefully it would be a simple fix. We were told they don't make the part for this particular unit anymore because of its age. It was original to our early nineties park model. The next best thing besides replacing something that still worked was to place a large cement block on top to decrease the rattling or shaking when the unit was running.

This summer when we turned it on during a predicted week-long heat spell, the racket it was making seemed worse, louder, even with the weight on top. It was also apparent that it was not cooling the house the way it used to. "Okay, let's take care of this," my husband said after hearing the unit as he walked several houses down the street.

Our next discussion consisted of how we could and have survived quite well without the use of air conditioning mostly—except on those sweltering humid nights that cause us to lose sleep.

Our discussion lead to Covid-19 and not knowing about his employment from day to day. "Maybe we should wait it out," I suggested. My husband was adamant that we shouldn't wait, even though we don't use the air often. It seemed like such a lot of money to spend in such uncertain times.

Since he still insisted, I called to get an estimate and possibly make the appointment, I expected a long wait because of the pandemic, however, the owner of the heating and cooling company answered and he said, "You're timing is perfect. We have a cancellation and can do the install on July third." I checked with my husband to see if he had changed his mind after I repeated the quote, and he said, "That's quick. Great. Schedule it."

So, three days later, two men showed up in the morning and replaced the unit. All went smoothly with the install, but when one of the men did a standard check of the furnace because the air conditioner is connected to the furnace's blower system and its ductwork, he discovered yet another problem—a more than substantial gas line leak within the furnace. There were lots of bubbles with a simple soap test. He said he could seal off the leak if we weren't going to use the furnace—or we could replace the part. He had one available.

I was so happy my husband was there to see the

problem. The installer who is also a volunteer fireman, said it probably had been a slow leak over a long time, maybe even a couple of years, and had grown larger with temperature and moisture fluctuations during the time our home is closed for the winter season.

He also said if we would have engaged our furnace this fall, it may not have ended well. The leak was at that much of a dangerous level.

It took a bit for all of that to sink in. What he was saying was that when we would turn on the furnace on one of those chilly autumn nights, which we always have—before the park closed on October 31, we could have blown up our home. If it didn't happen then, it could have happened when our maintenance man opened our home in May and tested the furnace. Either scenario made my blood run icy.

That's the moment when I could hardly breathe through the realization of this life-and-death situation. The emotions, tingles, and usual warmth took over my body as the reality of what he'd said settled in. All I could think was *There it is...the smoke detectors dream.* Now it made perfect sense.

We could have blown ourselves and our dream-come-true lake house up, along with our closest wonderful neighbors. A couple of years of a slow leak, hmm-m. Two years before was when I'd had the dream and thought it was connected to my cancer. At that time, I had checked all the external gas lines, but I hadn't thought to take the cover off the front of the furnace unit to check inside.

I'm thrilled we have a new air-conditioner and so happy my husband was adamant about getting one, even though we both complain we don't like air. But even more important, I am feeling blessed beyond measure to be alive, along with my husband, wonderful neighbors and a tremendous maintenance man. Because of this divine timing and true miracle, I'm here to tell you this story and to finally put that last piece of the rebus puzzle in its place. All is well and as it is meant to be. I'm not finished in this life yet.

I know there are an infinite amount of stories to write and miracles to celebrate!

Another Special Sign from Faith

Each day as a radiation patient, you lay on a not-so-comfortable metal table as they adjust and measure your body to have you in the perfect position so the radiation enters only the area to be treated. To help do this accurately, several laser lights are attached to the walls and the ceiling around the room. When turned on, these lines form a graph over the body lying on the table. Two or three people check the placement of lines and call out random numbers to make sure that the part of the body to be radiated is in perfect alignment with the tattoos for the treatment.

Located above my head was such a laser light. It was the one I stared at every day for a few moments while the measurements were being taken. When the lasers were turned off and the accuracy of the numbers were all verified is when the radiation would be administered by a separate machine.

The sharp green lights within the laser formed the perfect shape of a butterfly. Every day before each treatment began, I thought of my friend Faith and all she'd had to go through with her battle of stage four cancer, and I knew that this butterfly was meant to calm and let me know she was there with me. I went through every treatment feeling relaxed because of Faith.

Thank you, my dear friend Faith, for still being with me. No one else saw this. I asked the radiation therapist if anyone had ever mentioned the butterfly to him. He shook his head. So, when I was done that day, I asked him if I could take a picture and show him what I saw before each treatment. He was amazed and said he could see how that would sooth me. He even laid on the table and agreed that it did indeed from that angle look like a shape of a fluttering butterfly.

Now I feel once again validated in my purpose of this life. Writing and sharing my experiences are absolutely what I am supposed to be doing. I feel the radiation was part of my life's synchronicity for me to make a difference in the lives of others, including my husband and my favorite nemesis. I try to remember sometimes that the way our lives unfold isn't always for or about us, but often it is to bring inner peace, comfort, understanding, and love to others. What I do know for sure is that God, the Universe, Faith, and the angels don't make mistakes. Whatever it is you call that higher power, our creator knew what I and the others surrounding me needed from their perspective. I am grateful!

As an extra blessing, I sold fifteen books at that office. It was like a miracle. Sometimes I sit at a craft sale for eight hours or an entire weekend and never sell a copy. All those sales came about because I believe the doctor had scribbled a note on my paperwork that I was a writer and a published author. To me, that wasn't the appropriate place to market books, so I didn't. But then again, I'm not in control of the Universe.

My very dear friend Faith has proven over and over that she is still, even though transitioned, by my side doing all she can to help me. She brings many smiles, comforts me, guides me in dreams and messages, and nudges me to be the best I can be in this earthly experience that we humans call life. She is the common *Love* thread of many of the synchronicities shared throughout this book with her name appearing over forty times.

Thank you, Faith, for helping me through it all. I loved you then, I love you now and I'll love you forever. Until we meet again…

Ponder: In retrospect, have you ever discovered the silver lining to something that you thought was tragic? What good came from something that you thought was devastating in your life? Did you say 'thank you' for the experience, however unpleasant it was for you at the time? Did it affect the people around you?

Chapter 14

The Lion's Quest

"Do not wish to be anything but what you are and do that perfectly."
~ *St. Frances De Sales*

The weirdest thing happened. It could be considered a coincidence, except I stopped believing in those as you already know. Now I only believe in divine timing. So, I'm calling this specific dream experience another twofer.

At my writing groups' meeting earlier in the week, we had discussed the deadlines and guidelines for the groups' second anthology book in the seasonal series. At that time, we were working on *Spring in the Mitten*. I didn't know if I could come up with a story submission for the book on time. This was when I didn't know what challenges lay ahead or how my body would react to the treatments. I had three entries in the groups' first book, *Winter in the Mitten*. I'd be happy if I could at least submit one story for this edition.

As I laid in bed that evening, I had tried to put all my cancer thoughts to rest and to think about something unique I could write that had to do with spring. Something that hadn't already been written about a million times.

While spring-like scenery and animals whirled in my brain, I fell asleep.

There has been much research done and many articles and books written about how our angels and deceased loved ones occasionally like to connect with us during our sleeping hours and give comfort or sometimes leave us messages.

I recall as a twelve-year-old girl that after my grandma had passed unexpectedly, she would enter my dreams the night before my date of birth and wish me a Happy Birthday, always accompanied by a hug. Even as a child, I never had any doubt that my grandma still loved me and felt it important for her to let me know.

I have also had some wonky dreams that I don't want to keep in my memory. However, there are times when I have woken up and felt the connection, the reality of the moment, and my senses let me know it was more than a dream. It's those nighttime visions, the ones that are so vivid in your mind that you still feel like you're in them, even when you are awake. That's how I felt on the morning of this dream.

As I sat on the edge of the bed—eyes still closed, the strong scent of the open fields and chilled spring air filled my nostrils and caused me to shiver. The vivid vision of what had seconds ago occurred replayed on the screen of my eyelids. *Was I still in the dream?* I remembered every tiny detail, but why? It felt so real, so vibrant, and it left a sense of urgency for me to understand its meaning. It didn't make sense to me. At this point I shook my head and opened my eyes. I needed to recognize these emotions. I knew there had to be a message or sign involved, not because I saw it but because I felt the intensity of it when I was fully awake.

I let my thoughts whirl for a bit before the frustration appeared. *For crying out-loud, it wasn't an exciting dream. It was...a dandelion. Why on earth would I dream about a weed—and with this emotional intensity?* Maybe I was supposed to write about the pesky dandelion for our spring anthology theme, since questioning what to write had been what my last thoughts were before drifting off to sleep. If I were to remember a dream, I would have preferred one about an angel message or maybe a hug from my deceased parents. *Why, when I finally dreamed a dream and could recall the details, would it be about an insignificant weed?*

The Dream

The dream began as a single plant waving its brilliant golden yellow head in a soft breeze, with emphasis on each petal pointed in my direction, as if to say, "Come... Follow me. I have more to show you." I approached the dandelion plant that was as large as a turkey platter and way taller than me. From where I stood, I could see that around the bend was an enormous field. There were acres and acres of identical gigantic plants in full bloom, although they were not quite as large as the single one that beckoned me. Their sunshiny yellow heads waved, aimed in my direction, prompting me forward and giving me the distinct feeling of *you have much to discover.*

I felt a bit confused, because dandelions aren't only about spring. They bloom all summer and into autumn. Who would want to hear about them anyway? Most people want them dead and gone. Hmm, I sensed there was a reason I remembered that dream. I needed to do a bit of research and see what might turn up. Maybe I could create a quirky spring poem for the anthology and my efforts wouldn't be a total bust.

In my continuing quest to use natural and organic remedies over the years, I'd never learned anything about dandelions. As the dream had prompted, I discovered I had a great deal to learn.

My mom used to pay me a nickel for every dandelion plant I unearthed in the front yard and placed in a brown paper grocery bag. That chore kept me busy for hours as a child, and at the end of the day, I felt rich. Another fun memory I have was when my friends and I would blow the white cottony seeds and make wishes in the field at the end of my block. I didn't realize it at the time, but I was creating good job security for myself, aiding in the growth of new dandelions. Right?

Inquiries

My first day of dandelion research had my mind reeling from all the health benefits this plant could provide. Every single part of the dandelion has natural healing qualities and had been used for those exact purposes for hundreds of years, often by royalty.

Here's a partial list of health benefits I have discovered about this wonderful so-called pesky weed —number ten being the kicker. *Message received!*

1) Blood purification
2) Cholesterol levels
3) Skin conditions—acne
4) Several digestive issues
5) Sugar control
6) Energy levels
7) Weight loss
8) Memory enhancer
9) Urinary tract infections
10) And…extensive studies have proven that it even kills some types of cancer cells

This natural medicine from the earth, the same one that was given to royalty for centuries, can be made into teas, salads, cooked greens, and I've heard dandelion wine is tasty too. In case you are wondering… No, I haven't tried that one yet.

Fun facts for tea making… The roots should be

harvested in the early spring and late fall when the plant is dormant, and the most energetic nutrients are in the root. The leaves should be harvested from later in spring through summer when the plants nutrients have moved above ground. Keep in mind that only plants that haven't ever been treated with insecticide should be used.

My Messages

This dream began with a magnificent, extraordinary, vivid, and detailed dandelion in the center of a field that called to me—or should I say 'roared' to me. I figured since I had thought about the spring entry before sleep, that this vision was for that purpose, but as I did the research, I knew and felt the familiar warmth and tingling sensations throughout my entire body and knew this dream was meant as an important message for the maintaining of my personal health. It checked off three health issues that I had struggled with in the past. I love natural preventative medicines and drink dandelion tea, both root and leaf daily. My body has a way of letting me know when I'm giving it something good and when I'm not. I'm sure you can all relate.

My second message: I created a quirky poem with a twist and felt it was perfect for my writing group's spring anthology called, "This Lion's Quest." This is a revised version from the anthology, *Spring in the Mitten,* by the Shiawassee Area Writers.

THIS LION'S QUEST

Pondering a springtime poem, with a sigh and a yawn
Maybe tonight I'll dream of a crocus or a fawn

My midnight muse wasn't what I had in mind
The Universe's signals mustn't have aligned

There stood a lion confident and proud
The breeze hoisted his mane as he bowed

Every sunlit strand shined in its own space
No one wants to meet a lion face-to-face

Regal was his stance, eyes created to astound
His stare conveyed his purpose to be profound

Expectant he stood with a fearless grin

There'd be no battle, I knew he'd win

His authority high, wearing dominion and splendor
My senses vibrated with a strong urge to surrender

This lion, a sight to see, had a plan to execute
He wasn't leaving without me, his newest recruit

My efforts were slow in his direction
Awareness flowed of a healing connection

Some landowners don't care if the lions stay or go
Others hunt to kill using poisons or other ammo

Records show this lion has provided medicine fit for
kings
You may ask, what does a lion have to do with such
things?

This dream, not connected to writing after all, but
about discovery
Who knew this lion could assist with my body's
health's recovery?

Due to my dream I am presently on the mend

Thanks to this lion I have a new lifelong friend

The sprout, stem, and bloom, are laden with nutrition
This lion aids in most any medical condition

Tests show he helps with digestion, and fortifies the
liver
Controls sugars, stamina, and is an all-around health
giver

Lowers cholesterol, purifies blood, and clears the skin
Heals urinary tract infections, I'd say it's a win-win

There's more—parts of this lion are memory
enhancers
It's now known to destroy specific cells of cancers

So, if you haven't already guessed
This 'Dandy Lion' *Dandelion* has conquered its quest

PONDER: Do you remember your dreams? Have
you ever felt that one or more has held a special
meaning or message? How did you know? What did
you discover?

Epilogue

From everything I've learned in over five decades of life, I've found the most important part of life is... *balance.* If you are off too far one way or the other, life will feel more difficult. To find the balance isn't always easy, though.

When I was diagnosed with cancer and discovered that there is a charted protocol the medical teams follow for each type and progression of the disease, I found myself feeling like a project number, not an individual. I had much to learn, however. In the end, once all the facts were in and I'd worked through my options, I decided on the surgery and the radiation and built a trust with all the doctors and nurses who were assigned to my case. I'm grateful for those who choose medical professions. I learned from the several years of caregiving I had done for my parents that it's not an easy job.

Going through this whole breast cancer journey, I have focused on remembering that balance is key — mind, body, and soul. I had both a medical and holistic team in place for the advanced healing of my body, mentally and physically. I had my loving church family for my soul and prayer support. I also had my immediate family and friends for a strong reinforcement in all three areas. What I hadn't counted on was the miraculous involvement of my deceased loved ones and the role they would play in this quest to conquer and heal my disease. They gave me complete confidence in knowing—all is healed, all is well, and we are never alone.

Without all these support teams to provide the balance I needed, I don't think I could have survived through the intense, emotional, life-changing mind and body challenges without going to that deep dark place of no return and further damage. I made it through this challenge with faith, hope, and copious amounts of love. I am beyond grateful!

My newest daily affirmation is, "I am healed. I am healthy. I am happy. I am a sacred being, and most of all, I am grateful for every circumstance and every person in my life."

Life keeps changing. That is one guarantee we can all count on, whether it's something wonderful or something we perceive as not so good. This too shall pass. Whatever the circumstance—health, relationships, or finances—it will change in perfect timing and sometimes goes beyond human understanding and/or expectation. I also believe it will be for our highest good, the highest good of a loved one, or for the highest good of the Universe.

I can only write and share from my own experiences and what I've learned from them, how I put my life's puzzle pieces together, and I hope that somehow you can find a way to do the same. I can share the feelings I experienced, the information I received, and how it came to me, but each person has their own rebus to solve in their own way. My best advice sounds simple. Pay attention and feed daily—your mind, body, and soul...and check your attitude about all three.

So, like the old Concentration game, piece by piece we uncover the tiny picture clues that show up in our lives frequently as we try to resolve our life's many puzzles. With each hint or sign, the message becomes clearer only when both you and the Universe are ready. From the nudges, clues, and answers that we receive, we create the most phenomenal stories and miracles of our own lifetime.

I am now on the cancer survivor's list!

Ring this bell,
Three times well,
Its toll to clearly say,
My treatments done,
This course is run,
And I am on my way.

Let's Celebrate Life's Miracles!

Finding Love in Unexpected Places

About the Author

Patti Rae Fletcher lives in Michigan with her husband. When life gets chaotic and it's time for a break her favorite past times are being by the water, fishing, writing, reading and relaxing to the sound of a crackling fire.

She credits her fifteen years of being employed in a school library as the key that turned her love of reading and literature into the passion she now has for writing.

Celebrate Life's Miracles is Patti's third book following, *Whoa Nilly a Nymph Grows Up (2019)* — A creative non-fiction children's book — and *This Sign Was Mine, Message Received! (2015)*

Patti has studied writing technique through college courses and conferences over the last two decades. She has publications in over two dozen magazines and in three anthologies.

She presently serves as the Vice President of the Shiawassee Area Writers (SAW) inspiring others to improve their craft and to keep writing.